HOLY HEROES

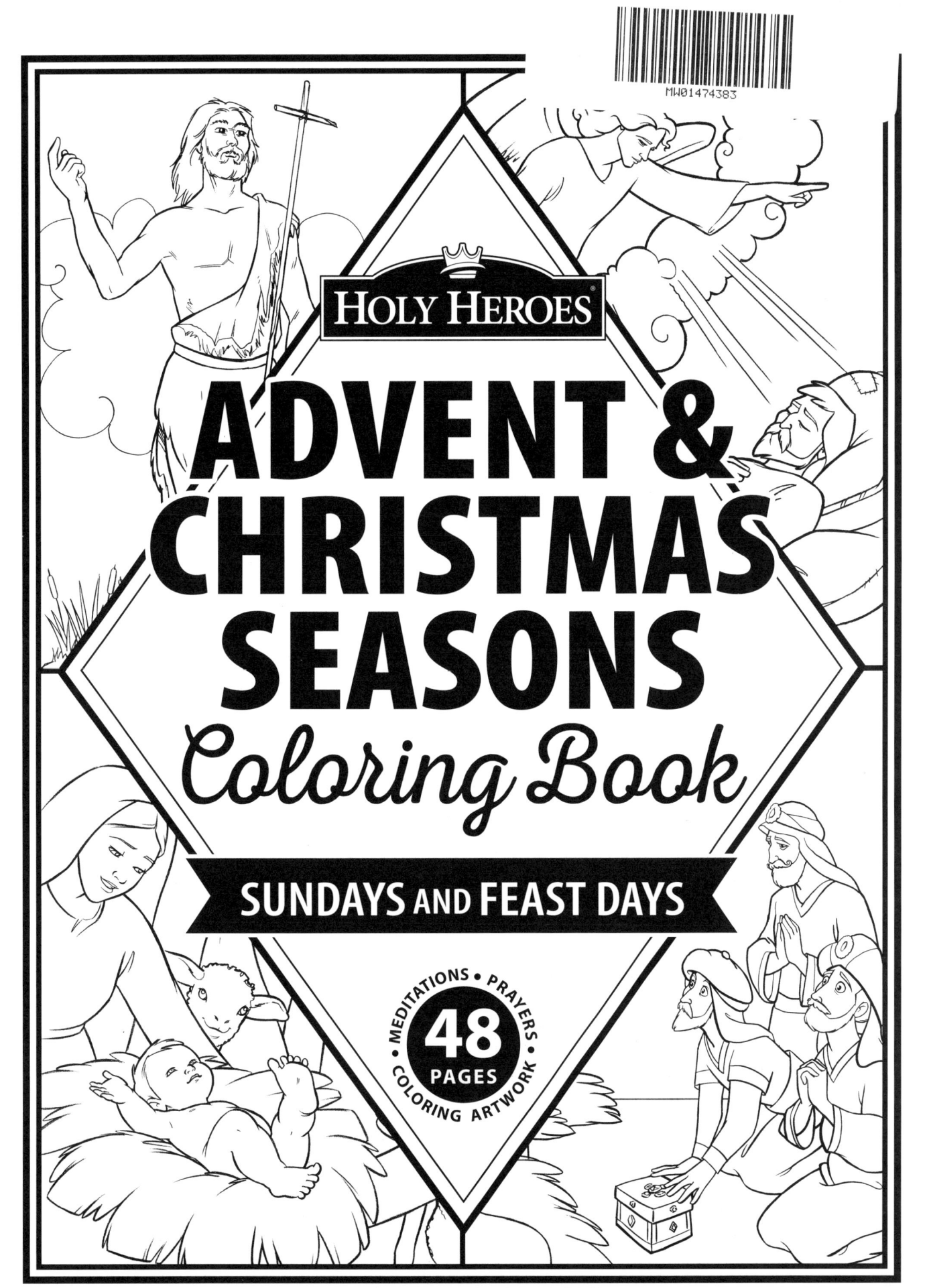

ADVENT & CHRISTMAS SEASONS
Coloring Book

SUNDAYS AND FEAST DAYS

MEDITATIONS · PRAYERS · COLORING ARTWORK

48 PAGES

©2019 Holy Heroes, LLC   ISBN: 978-1-936330-88-1

What is Advent?

The Advent Season is the beginning of the Church calendar. It is a time of penance and preparation. We save the parties for the Christmas season when we can truly celebrate the arrival of the Baby Jesus.

During Advent, the Church refrains from praying the *Gloria* during the Holy Mass, because "Glory to God in the Highest" (the first words of the *Gloria*) are what the angels proclaimed to the shepherds on the night of Christ's birth. By omitting this prayer during Advent, the Church helps us to prepare more consciously for the Christmas celebration, when we will once again sing the *Gloria* together with the angels, who first announced the birth of Christ.

Violet is the liturgical color of the Advent Season and symbolizes penance and preparation. While the total number of days in Advent changes each year, there are always four Sundays in the season. For the First, Second, and Fourth Sundays of Advent, the priest wears violet vestments. But for the Third Sunday of Advent, the priest wears rose vestments as a symbol of hope and joy. For this reason, the Third Sunday of Advent is called *Gaudete Sunday*, which means "rejoice" in Latin. On that day, the Church rejoices to be more than halfway to Christmas!

Some fun family traditions for Advent include lighting Advent candles, making a Jesse tree, and filling a sacrifice manger for Baby Jesus. You can find videos and instructions for all these fun activities (and more) online at **www.HolyHeroes.com/AdventAdventure**.

***Advent Adventure* is completely FREE, so be sure to sign up!**

First Sunday of Advent Second Sunday of Advent Third Sunday of Advent Fourth Sunday of Advent

_____   _____   _____   _____

Advent Candles Coloring Art

Color one lighted candle for each of the four Sundays in Advent
and write their dates on the lines above.

The First Sunday of Advent

Jesus reminds us to "be watchful," to "stay awake," and to "be prepared" to welcome Him into our lives at all times and especially during this season of Advent. We wait joyfully for the Lord, and by our daily prayers and works of charity we get ready for Jesus to return at the end of our lives and at the end of time.

PRAYER

Father, in You I place my trust. Let me be strong in my faith and remain watchful for the coming of Jesus. Help me to prepare well for Your Son's coming at Christmas and His final coming at the end of time. Amen.

Like Noah, we trust in God and wait patiently on Him.

Saint Francis Xavier

December 3

St. Francis Xavier spent his life as a missionary spreading the Catholic faith. Inspired by his friendship with St. Ignatius of Loyola, St. Francis Xavier became a Jesuit priest. His mission work took him as far as India and Japan in his efforts to bring people to Christ. He was canonized by Pope Gregory XV on March 12, 1622, and he is the patron saint of missions.

PRAYER

Jesus, help me to be bold in my Catholic faith to help bring others to You. Let me follow St. Francis Xavier's example and never falter in my love for You. Amen.

St. Francis Xavier, Jesuit Missionary

Saint Nicholas

December 6

St. Nicholas was the Bishop of Myra in the third century A.D. He was known for his immense generosity and kindness to the poor and needy. He was persecuted for his faith under the Roman Empire and was even exiled and imprisoned during his life. He is the patron saint of children and sailors.

PRAYER

Lord, I humbly ask You to protect me in all dangers through the prayers of St. Nicholas. Guide me so I may reach Heaven like St. Nicholas and join the Communion of Saints. Amen.

St. Nicholas, Bishop of Myra

The Second Sunday of Advent

Before Jesus began His public ministry, His cousin, John the Baptist, prophesied of His coming. John told his followers, "Repent, for the Kingdom of Heaven is at hand!" John wore clothing made of camel's hair and his diet consisted of locusts and wild honey. Many came to him to be baptized in the Jordan River—including Jesus!

PRAYER

Jesus, help me to follow St. John the Baptist's preaching and repent and prepare my soul for Your birth at Christmas. Help me make You happy with my prayers and sacrifices during this Advent. Amen.

**John the Baptist,
prophet and cousin of Jesus**

Get even more to color at:
HolyHeroes.com/LifeOfJesus

The Immaculate Conception of the Blessed Virgin Mary

December 8 or 9

In 1854, Pope Pius IX clarified the Catholic teaching on the Immaculate Conception, saying, "The most Blessed Virgin Mary was, from the first moment of her conception, by a singular grace and privilege of Almighty God and by virtue of the merits of Jesus Christ, Savior of the human race, preserved immune from all stain of Original Sin." Today, we celebrate Mary's preservation from Original Sin.

PRAYER

Father, I rejoice in You because You have protected me and wrapped me in the mantle of Your justice and mercy. You are the joy of my soul, and like the Blessed Virgin Mary, I will trust You forever. Amen.

Mary as a child with her parents, St. Ann and St. Joachim

Our Lady of Guadalupe

December 12

In 1531, Our Lady appeared to St. Juan Diego and asked him to have the bishop build a chapel in her honor. When the Bishop refused to believe him, Our Lady told Saint Juan Diego to climb to the top of Tepeyac Hill and pick the flowers he would find growing there. When St. Juan Diego presented the flowers to the Bishop, an image of Our Lady of Guadalupe miraculously appeared on his tilma.

PRAYER

Jesus, Your mother, Mary, appeared to humble St. Juan Diego and asked him to deliver a message for her. Help me to be as obedient as St. Juan Diego today and every day. Amen.

St. Juan Diego obediently accepted Our Lady's message to the Bishop.

Get even more to color at:
HolyHeroes.com/JuanDiego

Saint Lucy

December 13

St. Lucy was a martyr in the early years of the Church. She vowed to devote her life to Christ and remain unmarried. When St. Lucy refused to marry a non-Christian, she was arrested and executed. During her life, St. Lucy would bring food to the Christians hiding in the catacombs, and since she needed both hands, she would wear a wreath of candles to light her way.

PRAYER

Father, through the prayers of St. Lucy, help me remain pure and loyal to You. St. Lucy did not falter in her love for You, even when threatened with death. Help me follow St. Lucy's example through my life. Amen

St. Lucy, virgin and martyr

The Third Sunday of Advent

John the Baptist continued to preach about the coming of the Messiah. Even when he was thrown in prison for doing so, he praised God. When Jesus heard of this, He said, "Amen I say to you, among those born of women there has been none greater than John the Baptist; yet the least in the Kingdom of Heaven is greater than he."

PRAYER

Jesus, today I rejoice in Your goodness! As we near the end of Advent and approach Christmas, I rejoice in Your love and care for me. Amen.

John the Baptist continued to praise God even in prison.

The Fourth Sunday of Advent

Angels play a big role in the Coming of Baby Jesus. It was the Angel Gabriel at the Annunciation who accepted Mary's "Yes" to be the mother of God. It was also an angel who visited St. Joseph in a dream and told him to take Mary as his wife. And it was a choir of angels who announced the birth of Baby Jesus to the shepherds! All these people trusted in God's messengers and welcomed Jesus to the world.

PRAYER

Father, pour forth Your grace into our hearts; that we to whom the Incarnation of Christ, Thy Son, was made known by the message of an angel, be brought to the glory of His Resurrection. Amen.

An angel of the Lord appeared to Joseph in a dream.

What is Christmas?

The Christmas Season begins with the Vigil Mass on Christmas Eve and continues through the feast of the Baptism of the Lord in early January.

While many Christian churches finish celebrating Christmas on December 26th, the Catholic Church celebrates the birth of Our Lord for an entire season that only begins with Christmas Day!

There are four separate Masses that celebrate the Christmas Solemnity:

The four Holy Masses of the Nativity of the Lord (Christmas)
    The Vigil Mass (December 24)
    The Mass During the Night (December 25)
    The Mass at Dawn (December 25)
    The Mass During the Day (December 25)

There are also many special feast days within the Christmas Season:

    Saint Stephen, First Martyr of the Catholic Church
    Saint John the Apostle
    Feast of the Holy Innocents, Martyrs for Christ
    The Holy Family of Jesus, Mary and Joseph
    Solemnity of Mary, the Mother of God
    Saint Elizabeth Ann Seton
    The Epiphany of the Lord
    The Feast of the Baptism of the Lord

The Holy Family at the Nativity

The Nativity of the Lord
The Vigil Mass
December 24

An angel appeared to Joseph in a dream and told him not to worry that Mary was pregnant. The angel said, "It is through the Holy Spirit that this child has been conceived in her. She will bear a son and you are to name Him Jesus." Since the father was supposed to name the children in the Jewish tradition, Joseph knew he was supposed to act as the father on earth to Jesus.

PRAYER

Father, as I wait in hope for my redemption, grant that, just as I joyfully welcome Your Only Begotten Son as my Redeemer, I may also merit to face Him confidently when He comes again as my Judge. Amen.

**For it is through the Holy Spirit
that this child has been conceived in her.**

The Nativity of the Lord
Mass During the Night
December 25 (Midnight)

Joseph and Mary were traveling for the census and when they arrived in Bethlehem, there was no room in the inns. But they found a stable, and it was here that Baby Jesus was born and laid in a manger. Together, the Holy Family and the animals spent that first Christmas in a stable.

PRAYER

Jesus, I rejoice in You Lord, for the Savior has been born in the world! Today true peace has come down to me from Heaven. Amen.

She gave birth to her first-born son and laid Him in a manger.

The Nativity of the Lord
Mass at Dawn
December 25

On the night of Jesus' birth, angels appeared to shepherds who were keeping watch over their sheep. The angels announced the arrival of the Messiah and the shepherds immediately said to one another, "Let us go, then, to Bethlehem to see this thing that has taken place, which the Lord has made known to us."

PRAYER

Father, today a light will shine upon me, for Your Son our Lord is born for the world; and He will be called Wondrous God, Prince of Peace, Father of future ages: and His reign will be without end. Amen.

The shepherds looking upon the Baby Jesus

The Nativity of the Lord
Mass During the Day
December 25

Jesus Christ came down to earth as a little baby to save all people. The Apostle John writes that, "The Word became flesh and made His dwelling among us, and we saw His glory, the glory as of the Father's only Son, full of grace and truth." Mary, Joseph, and the shepherds were the first people given the privilege of looking at the Face of God on earth.

PRAYER

Father, let me rejoice in Your Son. As I celebrate Christmas, help me to remember Your generosity to me by sending Your only Son to save the world. Help me love Him as You do! Amen.

The Baby Jesus on Christmas morning

Saint Stephen

December 26

St. Stephen was the first martyr of the Catholic Church. He was one of the seven deacons ordained by the Apostles in the early days of the Church and was put in charge of looking after the daily needs of the Christians. Powerful Jewish leaders, angered by St. Stephen's preaching, accused him of committing blasphemy and condemned him to death.

PRAYER

Father, the gates of Heaven were opened for St. Stephen, who was found to be first among the martyrs and therefore is crowned triumphant in Heaven. Help me to follow his holy example and join him in Heaven. Amen.

St. Stephen, First Martyr of the Catholic Church

Saint John, the Apostle

December 27

St. John was the youngest of Jesus' twelve Apostles and is often referred to as "the disciple whom Jesus loved." One of Jesus' last words was to ask St. John to take the Blessed Virgin Mary into his home. St. John is one of the four Gospel writers. He was the last Apostle to die and the only one to die a natural death.

PRAYER

Father, St. John reclined on Your Son's breast at the Last Supper and spread the words of life throughout all the world. Help me to follow St. John's holy example today. Amen.

St. John, called "the disciple whom Jesus loved"

Feast of the Holy Innocents

December 28

When the Three Wise Men told King Herod the new King of the Jews had been born in Bethlehem, Herod became insanely jealous. He commanded that all baby boys under the age of two in Bethlehem and the surrounding area be killed, hoping the new King of the Jews was among them. The baby boys killed by Herod are called The Holy Innocents and are the first martyrs for Christ.

PRAYER

Father, the Holy Innocents were slaughtered as infants for Christ, Your Son; spotless, they follow the Lamb and sing forever, "Glory to you, O Lord." Amen.

The Holy Innocents, first martyrs for Christ

The Holy Family of Jesus, Mary and Joseph

First Sunday after Christmas

The Holy Family of Jesus, Mary and Joseph is a model for all Catholic families. Today's Mass celebrates the Holy Family and all families who are striving for Heaven. This is a good time to thank God for your family and think of how you can better help all your family members get to Heaven.

PRAYER

Father, You gave me the shining example of the Holy Family. Graciously grant me the ability to practice the many virtues Jesus, Mary, and Joseph portrayed through their lives. Amen.

The Holy Family at home in Nazareth

Solemnity of Mary, the Holy Mother of God

January 1

Mary was the person closest to Jesus on earth. When He was first born in Bethlehem, Mary watched as people came from near and far to pay homage to her baby son. St. Luke writes in the Gospel that, "Mary kept all these things, pondering them in her heart." She is an example of how Catholics should ponder the Word of God in our hearts as well.

PRAYER

Jesus, Your Mother, the Blessed Virgin Mary, is the perfect example of holiness for me to follow. Through her intercession, help me be made worthy of reaching Heaven. Amen.

In Heaven, Mary is still the mother of Jesus

Get even more to color at:
HolyHeroes.com/LifeOfJesus

Saint Elizabeth Ann Seton

January 4

St. Elizabeth Ann Seton was the first person from the United States to be canonized. After her husband's sudden early death, St. Elizabeth converted to the Catholic faith along with her five children. After persecution from her extended family due to her newfound faith, St. Elizabeth and her children moved to Maryland where she founded the Sisters of Charity of St. Joseph and opened a school.

PRAYER

Father, in St. Elizabeth Ann Seton's example, I see a wise woman who feared the Lord and walked in the right path. Through her holy intercession, grant me the same virtue today. Amen.

You can still visit the Mother Seton House and Historic Chapel in Maryland!

Get even more to color at:
HolyHeroes.com/Seton

The Epiphany of the Lord

First Sunday after January 1

Following the star of Bethlehem, three wise men (also known as Magi) came from the East in search of the King of the Jews. After a long journey, they finally arrived at the resting place of the star above the Holy Family. Immediately, the Magi fell to their knees and offered Jesus gifts of gold, frankincense and myrrh.

PRAYER

Father, the three wise men travelled a great distance to pay homage to Jesus. May I always be willing to follow their example and go to You, even when it is hard or difficult. Amen.

The Three Magi: traditionally known as Balthasar, Melchior, and Gaspar

The Baptism of the Lord

Sunday after the Epiphany

Jesus arrived at the Jordan River where His cousin, John the Baptist, was baptizing people. When Jesus first asked to be baptized, John refused, saying that Jesus did not need to be baptized. But after Jesus asked a second time, John was obedient. When he baptized Jesus, God the Father spoke from Heaven, and the Holy Spirit descended like a dove.

PRAYER

Father, after Jesus was baptized, the heavens were opened, and the Spirit descended upon Him. May I fulfill Your command to "Listen to Him" in my daily life. Amen.

The Baptism of Jesus in the Jordan

Get even more to color at:
HolyHeroes.com/LifeOfJesus

Get more coloring pages like the sample below plus FREE Mass Quizzes for the rest of the year at HolyHeroes.com/MassPrep!

Second Sunday in Ordinary Time

HOLY HEROES MASS PREP

John the Baptist saw Jesus coming toward him and said, "Behold, the Lamb of God, who takes away the sin of the world. He is the one of Whom I said, 'A man is coming after me who ranks ahead of me because He existed before me.' I did not know Him, but the reason why I came baptizing with water was that He might be made known to Israel."
(John 1:29–30)

©2019 Holy Heroes LLC. All rights reserved.